ADVENTURE

ADVENTURE

Kiki Adebola

VANTAGE PRESS
New York

Published by Vantage Press, Inc.
516 West 34th Street, New York, New York 10001

Manufactured in the United States of America
ISBN: 0-533-11349-0

Library of Congress Catalog Card No.: 94-90719

9 8 7 6 5 4 3 2 1

To Jesus
My wife, Sandra
My daughter, Ayo
My son, Kola

To all of yesterday's charm
And for tomorrow's convenience
As well as for those
Who can at times hear
That quiet voice within
Even in the midst of disquiet

Unless the Lord builds this house
those who build it
labor in vain.
Unless the Lord watches over the city
the watchmen stand guard in vain.

—Ps. 127:1

Contents

Part III: Springs of Adventure

Preface

That being may safely venture
who is so very well guided
by the power of God
that it does not go astray.

—Author

We all have a place with life. We are all created for life. No matter what or where we are, there is more for us. There is also more in us. The purpose of our being is to expand and unfold our innate potentials and abilities for the glorification of God. This we must not only recognize, but we must also acknowledge, experience, and express. Not that there is a predestined way it will come about, or time, or place, but it must come. The without of us must ultimately become the within. There will forever be within us a ceaseless urge to find truth and fulfillment, and to understand the unknown.

At heart, everyone is an adventurer. The adventurer is not outside of us, it is within us. However, the adventuring spirit within contests with the social person we are obliged to be. Like a bird we are born to be free, yet we go about our lives making cages for ourselves. We are born to venture with a meaning for our coming, but the nature of self is so strong that we venture along clinging to the things of this world and all the while refusing the fullness of life.

Sometimes, nothing short of a crisis (as in my case) will shake us out of our ruts and spur us on to let go and let the power of God come into and work in our lives. When the ties that bind our minds are broken by the power and spirit of God, the real us is introduced. Only then do we truthfully thrust forward toward meeting and achieving our full potential and fulfilling the meaning of our coming and adventure.

All of us human beings need light for our bodies. But we also need light for our minds and spirit. The light we need to make us see, as whole and complete true human beings, lies in the truth and the word of God.

It is with this in mind that I, over the years under inspiration, have written and compiled this book that contains the experiences and lessons of my adventure in life. It is my greatest hope that this book will be indispensable to those who can read between the lines.

Some parts and pieces used in this book have been collected without due credit given. This is so because their sources have long since been forgotten.

This book also happens to mark the beginning of my new life. It is the affidavit of God representing His work and power in my life. Without Him, this would not have been possible.

Here is a sigh to those who love
and a smile to those who hate
and whatever sky is above me,
here is a heart for every fate.

Introduction: Adventure

All life comes from God
All life returns to God
All life lives in God
All life belongs to God

The adventure of life
Is the venture of truth
And the venture for truth
Is the experience of adventure

Truth is life
Life is reality
Reality is truth
And truth is absolute

Life is an adventure
That we venture but once
What we do with our adventure
Determines our eternal life or death

On that day of judgment
Every knee will bow, and
Every tongue will confess
That truth is absolute

The secrets of adventure
Belong to God
But the reality of venture
Belongs to the adventurer

This is the wish of God
That we venture our lives nobly
Such that the true nobleness
That lies in other adventurers
Though sleeping but not dead
Will be able to rise in majesty
To meet our own with modesty

ADVENTURE

PART I

Kiki's Raps

Introducing Kiki

My name is Kiki
That is who I am
One and only Kiki

K is for kisses
I is for improvement
K is for kindness
I is for inspiration

To say that I ain't modest
Will be an understatement
Underneath my shyness
Resides my coolest self

My life quest is righteousness
And living a fruitful adventure
I've got a fresh radiation
And my spirit is really tall

On top of it all
It's got to be understood
That I am an adventurer
Who is ever evolving
With a heart full of love

K is for kisses
I is for improvement
K is for kindness
I is for inspiration
That is who I am
One and only Kiki

Inside of Me

I am a spiritual being
On an adventure of life
All I want before my time
Is to give my best to life

I come from beyond
To beyond I am bound
A being among beings
A soul among souls

I know about landscapes
Of mountains and valleys
The flow of rivers and streams
The color of flowers and trees

I've seen many mountains
Crumble into the seas
I've also seen beautiful birds
Flying high across the skies

I know about the desires
Of human wants and needs
But I am content to know
That true love resides in me

I cast all of my lot
With love and goodness
And so I shall die
With my hope in God

Within Me

I seek within myself
A special space for me
Where I may find quietude
And be in tune with God

At any day or night
At any hour or time
There I blend with joy
Into the sea of eternity

I seek within myself
A special space for me
Where I can relax myself
And be in tune with God

That special space for me
Is deep within myself
Where the divine spirit of God
Resides and reigns supreme

Thoughts

My name is Kiki
My age is not important
My height is just right
And my sign is Aquarius

My hobbies are mainly
Music and writing
The greatest time for me
Is cooling out with nature

My past experience with darkness
Brings this truth to my mind
That though darkness rules for a time
The shine of light has no end

My most important zeal
Is to live my life for God
And wishing that all humanity
Will come together as one

My Writing

If you can read the words
Written in between the lines
It is my writing you read

If you can see a house
Built upon a solid rock
It is my writing you see

I love you, my writing
For when my soul is troubled
Into you I come running
That I may find solace

You know me so well
O you my writing
That deep inside of you
I can love and be loved

Bring out your very best
O this my blessed soul
That my writing and I
May have a fruitful adventure

Kiki's Raps

1. I celebrate myself
   And so
   I rap of myself

2. I believe in God
   And I also believe in Jesus
   As my personal Lord and Savior

3. I am a spiritual being
   I live in a spiritual world
   And I will forever be
   Governed by spiritual principles

4. Each of Kiki's raps
   Is just one of the windows
   Into my inner heart,
   My mind, my self

5. I know I sometimes
   Contradict myself
   "I am a large man
   Of many volumes"

   —Walt Whitman

6. In the midst of winter
   I suddenly realized
   That there was in me
   An invincible summer

7. The sound of silence
   Says what I think

8. Writing has not only been
   A purpose with me,
   It has now become my passion
   As well as a sanctified home

9. I know the Bible is holy
   Because it never ceases
   To know me better

10. I am, and know, and will
    I am knowing and willing
    I know myself to be and will
    I will to be and know as well

11. I will chide no one
    But myself
    Against whom
    I know most faults

12. I am a man of hope
    I am a man of dreams
    I am a man of reality
    I am also a man of today

13. I always try to be me
    To be at peace with myself
    Regardless of who, what
    And how others are

14. I am who I know I am
    Goodness resides in me
    My shortcomings notwithstanding
    I am much better than my worst

15. I have no regrets whatsoever
    Of my past and ignoble life
    Of drug addiction and homelessness
    Because I've learned from my experience

16. I do not think of myself
    As being better than anyone
    In the eyes of God
    Everyone is equal

17. I can be very optimistic
    But I am also very pragmatic

18. My approach to life
    Is to make hay
    While the sun shines
    One day at a time

19. The knowing of myself
    Is the knowing of humanity
    Even though everyone is unique
    We are all very much alike

20. I've always felt that
    The greatest reward for doing
    Is the opportunity to do more

21. I always get better
    When I argue alone

22. I have never experienced
    Any type of adversity
    Which I've not in the end
    Seen was for my own good

23. The longer I live
    The more beautiful and meaningful
    Life becomes to me

24. I've come to find myself so alive
    With the freedom of living
    So I give thanks and praises
    To God for His gift of life

25. My strength
    Is made perfect
    In my weakness

26. I cannot separate myself
    From my writing
    My writing is me
    And I am my writing

27. I haven't forgotten my home
    It is always on my mind
    I do feel homesick at times
    There is no place like home

28. I've done some things in my life
    That were not the best of me
    I cannot share them with everyone
    Some things are better left unsaid

29. I have no racism in me
    I have total love and respect
    For all human beings
    Regardless of color or creed

30. I don't expect others
    To live up to my expectations
    Neither should they expect me
    To live up to theirs

31. I write in my extreme moods
    Sometimes when I'm in a bad mood
    Sometimes when I'm in a good mood
    But I am at my best
    When I'm in fine-tune with the spirit

32. Adversity as I've found out
    Has the effect of eliciting talents
    Which otherwise in prosperous circumstances
    Might have perhaps lain dormant

33. I am as bad as the worst
    But gracious thanks to God
    I am as good as the best

34. The light inside of me
    I know will be with me
    Long after my time is done

35. I am never less at leisure
    Than when at leisure
    And I am never less alone
    Than when alone

36. I always endeavor to
    Subdue circumstances to myself
    And not myself to circumstances

37. I am a citizen of the universe

38. My conscience is my crown
    In contented thoughts lies my rest
    My heart is happy all over
    And my bliss is deep within

39. My mind and I
    Are more than friends
    Yet we sometimes
    Do not understand each other

40. I prefer death to lassitude
    I never grow weary
    Of serving others
    In any way I can

41. Deep inside of me
    All fear is gone
    Only the love of Christ remains

42. In my state of freedom
    I have been disembodied
    Of materiality

43. There are good and bad times
    Tell me who needs the bad times
    But they are always there

44. The life I once lived
    As a homeless drug addict
    Was the lowest I've ever been
    As well as my worst nightmare

45. Only so much do I know
    As I have lived

46. I've never known a companion
    That is so companionable
    As solitude itself

47. Things haven't always been fine with me
    I've always had to overcome hard times
    Though things do sometimes look dismal
    I've always somehow survived

48. I will die adoring brightness
    Loving my friends at heart
    Never hating my enemies
    And ever detesting darkness

49. As I prayed
    I thought that prayer was talking
    But as I continued to pray
    The more I became still
    That until in the end
    I realized that prayer is listening

50. As long as I live
    I'm still on an adventure

51. I am a being of goodness
    Lord knows I love goodness
    I will never be so stupid
    As to mistake goodness for weakness

52. While asleep
    I dreamt life was beautiful
    But when I woke up
    I found out life is a duty

53. I give freely to life
    And life itself
    Gives freely to me

54. I am only one
    But still I am one
    I cannot do everything
    Still I can do something
    I will not refuse to do
    That which I can do

55. I have the simplest of tastes
    Goodness and righteousness
    Are my satisfaction

56. Nothing can work me damage
    Other than my very self
    Any harm that I sustain
    I carry about with me
    I am never a real sufferer
    But by my own faults

57. I am always at a loss
    To know how much to believe
    Of my own adventure

58. I see miracles every day
    I am a miracle myself

59. One of the best things
    That has happened to me
    Is the second chance I now have
    To live rry life over again

60. I am not ignorant
    Of my history and roots
    I am consciously aware
    Of my being black

61. When I reflect upon
    The tracks of my life
    I cannot help but acknowledge
    That I've been blessed big time

62. From day to day
    It becomes clearer to me
    That there is no other fulfillment
    Than in living completely for God

63. I don't dwell in yesterday
    Neither do I wait for tomorrow
    I am a man of today
    No one is promised tomorrow

64. In the new life I live
    I live by faith in Christ
    And not by sight

65. I've been all over the world
    From the North to the South
    From the East to the West
    I've also been into me

66. I am more matured
    More whole and complete
    Than I was yesterday
    But I'm still evolving

67. Two of the many qualities
    That I like about myself
    Are that I have a grateful heart
    And a humble spirit

68. I personally dislike imps
    All they do is vex my spirit
    They're such unpleasant creatures

69. I bless my writing
    And my writing blesses me

70. My wishes and prayers
    Are to live a life of
    Submission and obedience
    To the will of God

71. Under the bludgeonings of life
    I got bloody and bruised
    But I remain unbowed

72. I pray in times of distress
    I pray in times of need
    I pray in times of abundance
    And whenever the spirit moves me to

73. I've wished countless of times
    That one could resign life
    As an officer or official
    Resigns a commission

74. I have over the years
    Learned to be content
    With whatever my lot is
    Rather than attempting to satisfy
    Insatiable wants and needs

75. I know of no sweeter thing
    Than to be a human being
    Among other human beings

76. In all that I do
    I'm always on the lookout
    For new and positive ideas
    To find their expression through me

77. I am suffocated and lost
    When I have not
    The bright and good feelings
    Of progress in sight

78. I have the disease to observe
    It is almost as good in me
    As daylight is in darkness

79. The evenings are never
    More beautiful to me
    Than when I've been pleased
    With the morning

80. All that I've seen
    And all that I've experienced
    Teaches me to trust in God
    For all that I've not seen

81. From a personal experience
    Disobedience is at first pleasing
    Then it grows to become easier
    Delightful, frequent, habitual
    And then confirmed
    It later becomes more impenitent
    Obstinate, and finally ruinous

82. I always try to preserve
    A certain integrity of mind
    Whenever I act ineffectively
    I then wait for another time
    When I can act more effectively

83. I pray that I have
    An economy that is suitable
    To my fortune in life

84. I love my calling with passion
    It is the meaning of my coming

85. I love my country
    More than other countries
    But I love my humanity
    More than my country

86. I affirm that I am keenly responsive
    To the power of God within me
    I harken to its guidance
    And I behold its good at work
    Through this marvelous medium,
    I am quickened and healed
    And my life is totally transformed

87. This is a fact for me
    That it is not so much
    Where I stand
    As it is towards what,
    And which direction I am moving

88. Of all that I love
    God comes first
    My family comes next
    Every other thing follows

89. Whatever I can become
    I am already

90. He gives not best who gives most
    But he gives most who gives best
    If I cannot give bountifully
    Yet I will give freely

91. I don't put my trust in humans
    Humans can always fail
    I put my trust in God
    God never fails

92. During my course of creativity
    I've gathered me a bouquet
    Of the flowers of others
    And only the thread that binds them
    Originally belonged to me

93. My thinking about writing
    Is to think well
    To feel, and to render well
    It is to possess at once
    Intellect, spirit, and taste

94. I am always aware
    Of the divine presence
    It is ever in me
    And I am secured in it

95. I have no lofty ambitions
    I don't marvel beyond my scope
    My desire is but tranquil
    Peaceful and fruitful adventure

96. Since God came into my life
    My life has not been the same
    I now have a new life to live
    And my prayers are being answered

97. Boredom as I've found out
    Is the most horrible of wolves

98. Regardless of age or time
    My writing is for posterity

99. I have a love for mankind
    But I dislike the institutions
    Of the dead unkind

100. I am as made by God
    And so I live in God

101. All my experiences in life
    Have led me to who I am
    I am extremely confident
    In who I am

102. Winter is in my head
But spring is in my heart

103. I would rather walk with God
In the dark
Than go alone in the light

104. All my prayer to God today
Is to make His will known to me

105. Ever since my inner kingdom
Became opened to me
All that I can see
Is the reflection of my being

106. Though I'm getting older every day
My writing keeps me younger

107. When I did well
I heard it never
When I did ill
I heard it ever

108. With an open mind and heart
I meet and make changes
And I am ever ready
For all new beginnings

109. I push forward with all I have
To meet my good with determination
Because I surely know that
Almighty God is with me

110. My truest measure of loving God
Is to love Him without measure

111. When I am no more
I hope it will be said
Though his sins were scarlet
His writings were read

112. My best way of getting even
Whenever someone does me wrong
Is to forget

113. Whenever I give
I give myself away

114. Fighting back
Is not my way
But if something threatens
What and who I am
I will then have no choice
But to take a stand

115. I once was homeless
And even then I had a home
Deep within my heart

116. Throughout my entire life
I've always learned
To mind my own business

117. What I like in a good author
Is not what the author is saying
But what the whispering is about

118. I know myself now
And I feel within me
A peace above earthly vibrations
That peace is a still
And a quiet conscience

119. I thank God for all my shortcomings
For through them
I have not only found myself,
I've found my work and duty
And I've also found my Savior as well

120. I flow into the vibes of others
Not only to know myself better
But that I may also be able
To express myself better

121. My hope in life
Is that someday
My good loving
Will come shining through

122. What constitutes
Goodness to me
Is what is right and true

123. From where I used to be
To where I am today
Has made me know
That we never stop growing
Until we pass away

124. One of the things
That I want to be
Is to be a prayer warrior
For the Lord

125. Interracial marriages to me
Transcend all barriers
That ignorance cannot overcome

126. I cannot be a friend
Until I first be one

127. There are times of my life
Where I wished of the possibility
Of winding back the time
So I could re-live my life over

128. Whenever I listen
To the music of life
Only then am I able
To join in the dancing

129. My adventure in life
Is not to remake myself
But to make the best
Of what God made me

130. Though I live in a dark world
The windows of my heart
Are wide open
Looking into another world
Where sunshine is forever

131. I am not afraid of tomorrow
For I have seen yesterday
And I love today very much

132. The happiness I share
Does not deplete my store
I freely give and find
That I have more to give

133. As long as I live
I shall always be
Myself and no other
But myself

134. Since becoming a parent
Parenthood has made me
Grow immeasurably

135. Being a husband
Has made me better
Understand what love is
To share oneself unconditionally

136. I came to the U.S.A.
In search of the American dream
What I found instead
Is the heavenly dream in Jesus

137. My spirit
Is more of a giver
Than of a receiver

138. I have a past to remember
I have today to live
With a future to mold

PART II

Songs of the Spirit

This is the day
Which the Lord
Has made;
Let us rejoice
And be glad in it

—Ps. 118:24

*   *   *

"Whenever I hear the sound of music I go into a state of merriment."

Music

Music is a prophecy
Of what life is to be
It is a rainbow of promise
Translated from seeing into hearing

Music is another dimension
It is a universal tongue
It washes away from the soul
The dust of everyday life

Music expels a heavy spirit
It preserves us in amity
It allays fierceness and anger
It is the best physic
For many a melancholy disease

Of all the gifts of God
It is the most magnificent
It heightens our devotion
And it gives delight with ease

And such are some of the inherent values of music to
all of mankind. One can safely say that a world without
music is dead. It can be compared to a body that is
classified as "clinically dead" in the medical profession.

Music, for what it is, is a part of the laws of nature
and growth. Even the earth makes its own sound as it
revolves in space. Since ancient times, music was thought
of as messages from God. And musicians were thought of

as the interpreters and organizers of the musical messages to all of mankind.

Music arouses the ideals of beauty and inspiration toward a perfect harmony that is undisturbed by human passions. It is also an expression eluding all earthly vibrations. Because of its transcendence, it can become a refuge of independence for the spirit.

Music is supposed to interpret lyrically one's evolving place in the environment. It is for this reason that the great works of geniuses are more than profound in their own respects.

In its special place among the divine gifts, music can become an instrument which humankind can use to overcome all earthly boundaries in order that we may go beyond frontiers. It is the will of God that this very noble art will always and increasingly elevate the spirit to an understanding of authentic human and spiritual values.

"If music be the food of love; Play on . . . "
　　　　　　　　　　　　　　　　—William Shakespeare

If It Was Meant to Be

If it was meant to be
We will not force it at all
We will not push it at all
It will happen so naturally

From the moment we meet
Our eyes will let us know
If what we see is real
And if it was meant to be

We will say what needs be said
Make the moves that need be made
We will commit ourselves to love
That it might reign supreme

And while we fly so high
On the sweet wings of love
Only love alone can reveal
What it has in store for us

If it was meant to be
We will not force it at all
We will not push it at all
It will happen so naturally

The Lady in My Life

You are my love
You are my life
You are my joy
The lady in my life

Everywhere I go
You're all that I see
When I sleep at night
You're ever in my dreams

I've crossed many oceans
Travelled through many lands
Praying with all my soul
For the blessing of your love
To come into my life

You are my jewel
You are my joy
You are my love
The lady in my life

Welcome into my life
All my nights are over
My new days have begun with
The lady in my life

As long as forever
Our love will shine brighter
I'll ever be there for you
The lady in my life

You are my twin
You are my fortune
You are my joy
The lady in my life

My Minnesota Queen

As long as I can remember
You've always been in my dreams
Even if it were to take forever
You're my queen I had to have

In our kingdom of love
That has come to be
I am the African king
And you're my Minnesota queen

You're nice and lovely
You're smooth and sexy
You're stylish and charming
You're my Minnesota queen

Your eyes are sky blue
They are as bright as sunshine
Your hair is golden brown
They are as beautiful as can be

Since you came into my life
My world is full of wonder
I love you with all my heart
So freely and completely

My Precious Love

You're much more lovely to me
Than all the roses in the garden
You're much more lovely to me
Than all the lilies of the valley

You're much more lovely to me
Than the rainbow in the skies
You're much more lovely to me
Than any love I've ever known

It seems like it's just yesterday
When we made up our minds
To share what we have today
To have a brighter tomorrow

I think we can make it now
The rainbow we've been waiting for
Has come to show us the way
That we might have a brighter tomorrow

You're much more precious to me
Than any diamond or gold
You're much more precious to me
Than anything in the world

Diamond in My Heart

Somewhere deep in my heart
There is this diamond
That I need to share
With someone like you

Every time you come around
You make me feel alive
Guess all I wanna do
Is share my life with you

This diamond in my heart
So charming as can be
Wanna share all of it
With someone like you

Should you wanna know
I'm not about playing games
I will give you the best of me
To make you wanna stay

This diamond in my heart
So charming as can be
Wanna share all of it
With someone like you

The Things You Tell Me

I love to hear you tell me
That you love me dearly
I love to hear you tell me
That I am your ecstasy

I love to hear you tell me
That I am your temptation
I love to hear you tell me
That I am your inspiration

I love to hear you tell me
Your love for me is unconditional
I love to hear you tell me
Your love for me is everlasting

It makes me know
That I ain't dreaming
It helps me be sure
You're the one for me

We are inside the rainbow of love
We have a new life to live
We are inside the rainbow of love
We have one destiny to experience

No One Else

There is no one else
Who is more worthy
Of all my love
Than your very self

There is no one else
Who can make me
More complete and whole
Than your very self

There is no one else
More meant for me
Than your very self
Sent from up above

You need to hear this
Over and over again
To make you reassured
And deeply secured in my love

I don't look for another
I have no regrets whatsoever
I am content with your love
You're the very one for me

100% Natural

Like a flower to a tree
Like harmony to melody
So you are one of a kind
You are 100% natural

You've got no artificial flavors
Neither have you artificial colorings
You've got no additives whatsoever
Neither have you any preservatives
You are simply one of a kind
You are 100% natural

What you are to me
Is what a woman should be
You're not in love with the world
You are 100% dedicated to love

Like a river flowing into the sea
Like a rainbow across the skies
So you are one of a kind
You are 100% natural

I give my life to you
With my best of affection
Under the natural protection
Of a 100% love

I Will Do Anything

If I have to wait another year
To get married to you
It will seem like a day to me
Because of my love for you

I will go through any fire
Climb the highest mountain
Do anything I have to do
To get married to you

What we got going between us
Is much higher and deeper
Much wider and stronger
Than any form of distraction

The way I feel about you
I wanna be married to you
Share all my life with you
And be faithful to our love

I will go through any fire
Climb the highest mountain
Do anything I have to do
To get married to you

I admire your patience and spirit
Your perseverance and commitment
Your grip and belief in love
And your withstanding the test of times

God's Time

One thing I know for sure
I've been more of myself
Since you came into my life
And turned everything around

I realized a long time ago
That I needed love in my life
So I went into the world
Attempting to fill the space within

I tried every trick in the book
If I could stumble upon love
But my best was never enough
My search was all in vain

When I least expected
You came out of nowhere
To fulfill all my dreams
And to complement my life

The way you materialized
And all that has transpired
Has taught me to be patient
And to always wait on the Lord

It pays to wait for love
Sometimes it takes a long time
But it is always on time
God's time is the best

Supernatural

What about love?
It's supernatural
Love on fire taken control
What about love?
It's supernatural
Love on fire taken control

I remember the day so well
From the crowd you stood alone
And what I saw that day
My eyes had never seen before

The closer I got to you
The faster was my heartbeat
My head started to spin around
And my body began to shiver

What about love?
It's supernatural
Love on fire taken control

The closer I got to you
I had to belt my feelings
From the sudden flow of emotions
To keep them from spilling over

Since the day of no return
I don't intend to look back
All that I've got to say
To you, baby, I surrender

What about love?
It's supernatural
Love on fire taken control
What about love?
It's supernatural
Love on fire taken control

Star of My Life

Baby, that look in your eyes
You're asking what's on my mind
You ought to know by now
You're the star of my life

You're the star of my life
That time cannot steal away
Astonishing you are to me
With you at last I'm home

In all that you do
You're always at your best
You've done so much for me
You're every wonder to me

Even when we become gray
I will love you more each day
Should our road become bumpy
Our love will lead us the way

You're the star of my life
I love so well
You're the star of my life
I love so well

Bye-Bye

Got to say bye-bye to you
Say bye-bye to your love
Reaction to your phony smiles
Reaction to your sad songs

Just because I've played the fool
You think your game is cool
It's about time you realize
Your style ain't the best of all

Got to say bye-bye to you
Say bye-bye to your love
Reaction to your phony smiles
Reaction to your sad songs

For every star that falls
A new one will glow
For every dream that dies
A new one will grow
So while my heart is still strong
Baby, another way is calling

Now our love is lost at sea
No one but us gets the blame
Now our love has gone away
It will never be the same again

Got to say bye-bye to you
Say bye-bye to your love
Reaction to your phony smiles
Reaction to your sad songs

Restless Heart

How long have I to wait
Before fairy tales become true
All I need is a miracle
To be on my way to freedom

How long have I to wait
Before time claims a heart
All I need is a miracle
To be on my way to freedom

Who can hear this restless heart
Waiting for one heart's desire
Who can hear this restless heart
Waiting for that day of freedom

Precious time, they say
Waits for no one
Heaven help those, they say
Who help themselves

I don't wanna spend my life
Living inside the hell of time
I wanna live all my life
Spreading one love over all

Who can hear this restless heart
Waiting for one heart's desire
Who can hear this restless heart
Waiting for that day of freedom

Sunshine

My sunshine is always shining
That's the way it has come to be
My sunshine is always shining
Giving me hope when the day is done

Half of nothing ain't much
Yet my sunshine is half of me
My sunshine is my blessing
Giving me hope when the day is done

Yes, I believe in blessings
With all that has happened to me
My sunshine is always shining
Giving me hope when the day is done

When the life gets so hard
The world will try to fool you
But if love is in your soul
Your sunshine will see you through

My sunshine is always shining
Brighter time after time
My sunshine is always shining
Giving me hope when the day is done

Your Kinda Love

Your kind of love
Is like a mirage
That seems to be there
But never was there

Your kind of love
Is like a shadow
That fades into gray
When the evening comes

Your kind of love
Is like the mice
That come out to play
When the cat is away

You call me honey
You call me baby
You call me sweetheart
That never was from your heart

If you want to keep my love
You got to make your love for me
Be like mine is for you
From the bottom of our hearts

Come into My Life

You're always in my dreams
I've kissed you a thousand times
Whenever we're closer than close
I wake up and you're gone

Come into my life
Come into my life
My love is waiting on you
Come into my life
My heart is waiting for you

Time and time again
You tell me to be patient
That the finer things in life
Are worth waiting for

Can't hold my tears any longer
Got to know what it will take
For me to win your love
For you to come into my life

Come into my life
Come into my life
My love is waiting on you
Come into my life
My heart is waiting for you

Your love is all I need
Don't make me wait forever
Just jump into my life today
And come set my spirit free

Tonight

Oh what a plan tonight
When the mood is right
Just you and me baby
Tonight is for our love

Tonight calls for ecstasy
For us to fulfill a fantasy
So relax in my tenderness
And meet me in paradise

We'll go through nothing less
Than a mind-blowing experience
For every little action
There will be a sweet reaction
To give us the satisfaction

Through the shadows of the night
Until the early morning dawn
We will find the pleasure of romance
Inside the embrace of love

Tonight is for our love
A night we've been waiting for
Now it has come and gone
It's a night we won't forget

Twinkling Stars

There is a place I see
Where twinkling stars are born
It is way beyond the skies
Where twinkling stars belong

I can see this place so well
It is so nice and pretty
It is way beyond the skies
Where twinkling stars belong

Every star born in this place
Glows and twinkles so bright
Up above the world so high
Like a diamond in the sky

I can see the place so well
It is so nice and pretty
It is way beyond the skies
Where twinkling stars belong

I know my day will come
When I'll become myself
I'll be twinkling like the twinkling stars
Up above the world so high
Like a diamond in the sky

Love Nest

East is East
West is West
You are the only one
That I love best

As deep as the ocean
As bright as sunshine
So is my love solution
So is my heart's devotion

Mountains may rise
Mountains may fall
But my love for you
Will always be there

I love your cookie
I love your pie
I will always love you
Until the end of time

East is East
West is West
May the sun shine best
On our chosen love nest

My Dearest Love

My dearest love
Is one who knows me
Better than anyone else
Other than myself

My dearest love
Does not play tricks
My love does not wink
Neither does she flirt

My dearest love
Is my best friend
A love to cry with
A love to laugh with

One whose spirit
Makes me happy
And one whose love
Means so much to me

My dearest love
What I find in you
Is the very best
That love could be

Weekend

The past weekend
We spent together
Is more than a preview
Of what tomorrow holds

How I feel today
Is like I never felt before
My commitment to you
Has more than doubled

The past weekend
And all the good time
We spent together
Is the best I ever had

Your juicy fruit to me
Was as hot as microwave
And your tasty cake to me
Was as sweet as sugar

Though my mind has long
Been made up on you
It's even more so
Now than ever before

December 1st, 1993

Baby, baby, we got a day
It's a special day for us
That day is coming soon
It is December 1st, 1993

Oh, what a day it will be
I can't wait for it to come
It's a special day for us
The day we're gonna get married

The day is December 1st, 1993
When we'll become husband and wife
It's a day of a new beginning
It's a day of no looking back

Oh, what a day it will be
For us to exchange marriage vows
A day to commit ourselves to love
And a day to consummate our love

I can't wait for it to come
It's a day I'm looking forward to
It'll be a special day for us
The day we're gonna get married

Never Ever

I'll never find another
To love me like you do
Your love is like a fantasy
Like a fairytale to me

People spend a lifetime
Looking for what we have
True love is every lover's prayer
Divine as it's supposed to be

All the things that you do
Only add more wood
And fan the fire of our love
To keep burning with no end

I'll always do all I can
To keep you loving me
I know what I have in you
I appreciate your love for me

I'll never find another
To love me like you do
Your love is like a fantasy
Like a fairytale to me

You're Always on My Mind

You're my heat
You're my fire
You're my passion
You're always on my mind

Ever since I fell for you
I can't stop thinking of you
There's no getting over you
You're always on my mind

Whenever you're close to me
Whenever you're in my arms
It feels like paradise to me
Nothing seems to matter anymore

You're my all in all and all
That I've ever been dreaming of
How I'm so happy to know
That your love belongs to me

Some things were meant to be
Baby, I wanna be with you
I know now without a doubt
That our love is meant to be

Eyes of Love

In your eyes
I can see all the magnificent
And yet the simple things of creation

In your eyes
I can see deep inside of you
And the answers to my questions

In your eyes
I can see the wonders of today
And the hopes of tomorrow

In your eyes
I can see a tree budding in spring
And the beautiful sight of blooming flowers

In your eyes
I can see love birds dancing in harmony
And singing sweet songs of melody

In your eyes
I can see the sunrise in the east
And the sunset in the west

In your eyes
I can see why we're so in love
And why love is so in us

Higher Calling

There's a higher calling
That everyone needs to answer
This is the highest of callings
To willingly work for the Lord

No one needs to contemplate
If this is for them or not
This is the highest of callings
Workers are needed for the harvest

We're living in the end of times
The signs are everywhere to see
The harvest is very plentiful
But the workers are few

There's no other calling so worthy
Neither is there anything else so satisfying
As willingly working for the Lord
Bringing Him the glory and praise

Surrender yourself to the Lord
And let His will take control
There's enough room for everyone
The reward is everlasting life

Love

Love is life
And life is love
Love is true
And truth is forever

Love is the one
And only way to life
There's no other way
Other than love itself

Love is patient and kind
Not wanting any to perish
But for every single soul
To come to repentance

It offers freedom of choice
Between eternal life and death
It respects the mind and will
And the decision of every soul

Love is content
With joy and satisfaction
Its satisfaction brings happiness
And in its happiness
There is contentment

What I've Found in You

What I've found in you
Brings a sense of freedom
What I've found in you
Brings the blessings of life

The endless and many ways
Not to mention the distance you go
To show your love for me
Takes my breath away

When I'm lost and insecure
With my blood pressure so high
Your love is my sure insurance
That makes me feel okay

What I've found in you
Brings a sense of freedom
What I've found in you
Brings the blessings of love

Baby, what I've found in you
Is beyond endless measure
You are my priceless treasure
That my new life is built upon

Whenever I'm with You

Whenever I'm with you
You turn my whole world around
Whenever I'm with you
You make me feel so alive

Whenever I'm with you
You fill my heart with joy
Whenever I'm with you
It's more than a déjà vu

Whenever I'm with you
You're more than my valentine
Whenever I'm with you
It's like a page from a love story book

Whenever I'm with you
You bring out the best of me
Whenever I'm with you
You make me feel all right

Whenever I'm with you
Love ceases to be like a dream
Whenever I'm with you
Love becomes so real to me

This Feeling

I can't get over this feeling
That I just can't hide
Never wanna lose this feeling
Of living inside your love

You need me
And I need you
You belong to me
And I belong to you

I never ever thought
I would care for someone
As much as I do for you
My love for you is so special

Among all you mean to me
You're the only one I'm thinking of
Among all you mean to me
You're the only one I'm living for

I can't get over this feeling
That I just can't hide
Never wanna lose this feeling
Of living inside your love

True Love

There is a place I know
Deep in the clear blue skies
Beyond the rainbow of time
Where true love has no end

In this place I know
There is plenty of sacrifice
Lots of patience and trust
With respect and understanding

Come take my hand and follow
Into the clear blue skies
Beyond the rainbow of time
Where true love has no end

In this place I know
Love is a two-way traffic
It cannot be bought or sold
It is so pure and real

I can see this place in us
It is full of hope and promises
Come take my hand and follow
Into the clear blue skies
Beyond the rainbow of time
Where true love has no end

I Believe

I believe in God Almighty
For He is all my life
He blesses my soul daily
In Him I put my trust

I believe in Jesus Christ
For He is the word of God
The lamp unto my feet
And the light of my life

I believe in miracles
For I am a miracle myself
I was freed from captivity
Of being a slave to sin

I have a new heart today
My life is totally transformed
God is working on me daily
Into whom He will have me be

I believe in God Almighty
For He is all my life
He is my rock and refuge
Whose words speak peace to me

Your Love

You don't have to tell me
How much you love me
Because you show it to me
By always finding a way
To blow my mind away

I can see it in your face
I can see it in your eyes
I can see it in your smiles
I can feel it in your kisses

I can feel it in your touch
I can feel it in your warmth
And in the way you hold me
Like you never wanna let go

Should I have to tell you
As much as I can say
My love belongs to you only
And I'll never leave you lonely

It took me a lifetime
To find a love like yours
It will take me a lifetime
To keep this love of yours

Wonderful You

Once upon my lifetime
All my dreams came true
To be blessed with a love
Of someone as wonderful as you

You're not asking for the world
I'm not asking for perfection
We are just as we are
Nothing more, nothing less

You're everything I've hoped for
You're everything I've ever wanted
You're everything I need
You're the one for me

No words can truly express
The way you make me feel
You make me feel brand new
Like a very sunshiny day

You remain the only one
And there'll never be another
Who will be able
To win my heart for keeps

Shine on Me

Shine on me
Shine on me
Let the shine of your light
Come shining on me

Shine on me
Shine on me
Let your shine inside of me
Be bright for all to see

I delight myself in you
That you may grant unto me
The desire of my heart
To dwell inside your shine

There is no other light
Other than your shine
There is no other sunshine
Other than your light

Shine on me
Shine on me
Let the shine of your light
Come shining on me

The Future

I took a walk around
My old stomping ground
I heard a voice say to me
God is working in my life

Take a look all around
Tell me what do you see
All that I can see
Nothing but the future

All the clouds that held me blind
Have been rolled away by the blood
What a good feeling to feel
God is working in my life

All that I can see
Nothing but the future
Firmly, slowly, but surely
God is working in my life

Everything Will Be All Right

When the going gets rough
And gets too tough to handle
Be like a rock standing firm
Everything will be all right

When all your hope is lost
And you can't find your dreams
Be like a rock standing firm
Everything will be all right

When the night gets so dark
And there is no sunshine at all
To light up your way
Everything will be all right

Beyond the roughest of times
There's ever the power of love
To let us know we're not alone
We're always under its care

Open the doors of your heart
That love may come inside
To heal your broken self
And make you whole again

Times of My Life

There was a time in my life
When I got so confused
I didn't know which way to go
My life came to a standstill

There was a time in my life
When I got lost in New York City
Way uptown and downtown
In the wilderness of the streets

There was a time in my life
When I was in desperation
I was in need of inspiration
I was heading for destruction

Now is a time in my life
When my peace is like a river
God is working in my life
And I owe it all to Him

Now is a time in my life
When my hope is in God
Greater is He in me
Than the one in the world

I Love You So

You're always in my heart
You're always in my mind
Baby, you need to know
That I love you so

From the very first time
I told you I cared for you
My love for you has grown
To where I can truly say
Baby, I love you so

I need your love always
For whenever I'm with you
I keep falling in love
Over and over again

You're always in my heart
You're always in my mind
Baby, you need to know
That I love you so

Loving you is so simple
You make me feel so special
I'll always be by your side
I'm so glad you're in my life

My First Love

The first time I knew you
There was something about you
That took time for me to know
You're my very first love

The first time I knew you
Love was all over you
Tomorrow was in your eyes
I found myself falling in love

The first time I held you close
I felt two hearts beat as one
The first time I kissed you
I felt our bodies shiver

If I have to live my life now
Without you with me daily
My life will be so empty
Living won't be so easy

I got this peaceful feeling
That you won't let me down
Believing in you that
You're my very first love

Good Day

I woke up this morning
I was feeling fine
I said to myself
It's gonna be a good day

I had a good dream
Of a brand new day
That the whole of today
Is gonna be a good day

My wife and I
We made sweet love
We said to ourselves
It's gonna be a good day

With breakfast in bed
Oh, so nice
Sunshine so bright
On a brand new day

We went to the movies
And to see a show
In a brand new day
On such a good day

Too Good to Be True

Baby, everything we do
The true love we share
And the way you make me feel
Is too good to be true

When we're walking so close
When we're in wonderland
That feels new every time
Is too good to be true

When I'm thinking about you
When I'm with you at home
And when you're in my arms
Is too good to be true

The good times we've had
The marriage we have coming
And the promises of tomorrow
Is too good to be true

Communicate

When we communicate (communicate)
Through that language of love
Something strange comes over me
That no word can express

It's the magic in your eyes
And the beating of our hearts
When we communicate
(Communicate)

When we communicate (communicate)
What we share is always new
What we feel is always true
Just as it is supposed to be

It's the feeling of your love
And the beating of our hearts
When we communicate
(Communicate)

It's the magic in your eyes
And the beating of our hearts
It's the feeling of your love
And the beating of our hearts
When we communicate (communicate)

Watching Eyes

Eyes are watching
Come the day of love
Eyes are watching still

The life we live today
Is full of iniquity
For wrong has become right
And right has become wrong

They offer the people democracy
With hopes of political solution
But it is a rhetorical hypocrisy
There's no salvation in mankind

Eyes are watching
Come the day of love
Eyes are watching still

When the little ones grow up
They add feathers to their caps
Who are the fools of liberty
While they subjugate equality?

Love is the only solution
To our troubled situation
For there ain't no other resolution
Other than such a conclusion

Aquarians

Aquarians are vibrant
Aquarians are dynamic
Aquarians are dreamers
They are ahead of times

They are born from Jan. 20th to Feb. 19th
They are often lonesome at heart
But they can make the sun shine
With even half a smile

Many have thought them crazy
While some can't figure them out
Many have thought them creative
But that's just the general rule
They are ahead of times

Aquarians are truth-seekers
Water-bearers full of love
They live their lives for goodness
And nothing else will do

Half of them is spirit all right
And the other half is only human
Made up of flesh and blood
And born to make mistakes

Strange Woman

She doesn't live by the rules
She loves to be wild and free
She knows every trick in the book
While diamonds are her best friend

She's been strange since ten
Running around with playboys
She schemes in her daydreams
While diamonds are her best friend

Strange woman
Who's the sucker tonight
Strange woman
I'm sorry for the sucker now

If you're in want of heart
Let her beauty shake you down
Very soon you will discover
It's a river of no return

Down to dust you will go
If you ring her bell tonight
Down to dust she'll go
Her house is bound to fall

Moonlight—Sunshine

Moonlight—Sunshine
Moon for night, sun for day
Ever shining that we may see
Don't take your shine away

The night has a thousand eyes
And the day has but one
Yet the light of the day dies
Away with the fading sun

The mind has a thousand eyes
And the heart has but one
Yet the light of a life dies
Away with the fading heart

Moonlight—Sunshine
Moon for night, sun for day
Ever shining that we may see
Don't take your shine away

As the seasons always show
Nature depends on your shine
In you we live in time
Don't take your shine away

Mystery Lover

You play hide-and-seek with me
Then act as if you don't know
I know you're somewhere around
My feel can pick your vibes

The message that you send
Is all I've ever wanted
When we come face to face
Our vibes will be of love

Mystery lover in my dreams
Oh no, don't be a tease
Tell me how to win your heart
Your love is long overdue

Good things come to those who wait
But not to those who wait too long
If this is a price I've got to pay
Let the means be worth the end

Every day by day
You're the one I'm waiting for
Make me your choice today
I'll be everything to make you stay

So Far (So Good)

So far (so good)
All my life
What I know and have
Is goodness and love

So far (so good)
All my life
I am growing every day
Into a better me

What I'm all about
Is goodness and love
Passing them unto others
Before my time comes

So far (so good)
All my life
I am willing to pay
Dues that need be paid

So far (so good)
All my life
What I know and have
Is goodness and love

This Is to You

You might be thinking
I don't love you no more
I haven't written to you
A love song so long

This is to you
To let you know
I still care for you
Like I'll always do

Sometimes it seems
That my love for you
Is on the wane
Too fast and so soon

If anything at all
My love for you
Is not only the same
But has grown stronger

I still care for you
More than I did yesterday
Much more even today
Enough unto forevermore

I Meant It

I meant it
When I said I do
Not for just that day
But forevermore

You are my love
You are my joy
You are my life
Nothing can change that

Obstacles will come
Difficulties will arise
To make us worry
But love is with us

I meant it
When I said I do
Not for just that day
But forevermore

Be secured in my love
As I am in yours
What we have between us
Will endure forever

Coming Train

Coming train
Coming train
I can see your light
At the end of the tunnel

I'm at the train station
Standing on the platform
Waiting for you to come
Take me home

Coming train
Coming train
I can hear you coming
Thundering down the tracks

My sweet home is Jerusalem
On top of Mount Zion
Where everyone is free
To be as one with love

Coming train
Coming train
I got to get on board
I'm on my way home

Blessed Charm

You're my charm
You're my prayers
And all my hopes
Of today and evermore

I've always known
You're the one for me
But today I know now
You're my blessed charm

You're my everything
I can ever hope for
Beyond my every doubt
You must be heaven sent

You're my charm
You're my prayers
And all of my hopes
Of today and evermore

I treasure you dearly
To wanna love you daily
Every day of my life
With my very best

Right Choice

I know I made you
My right choice
Just as you made me
Your right choice

Everything we do
We do with love
To let us know
We made the right choice

We are so alike
In spite of our differences
We are so compatible
Like hand and glove

You're always there
Whenever I need you
I'll ever be there
Every step of the way

As the days pass by
The more I begin to see
We made the right choice
To be with each other

Your Titles, My Words

IF IT WAS MEANT TO BE
is where and how it all began
(followed by **THE LADY IN MY LIFE**)

MY MINNESOTA QUEEN
was written to remind me
that you are my African King
and ours is a kingdom of love

Since the very beginning I have come to know
that you are **MY PRECIOUS LOVE,**
the **DIAMOND IN MY HEART**

THE THINGS YOU TELL ME
serve to strengthen our bond
because I know the words
are actions themselves

There is **NO ONE ELSE** but you
in my heart, in my mind, in my life,
nor ever will there be

What you see me as,
I too can say for you
that you are **100% NATURAL,**
just as I would prefer you to be

It was **GOD'S TIME** which drew us as one
and in this **SUPERNATURAL** love we share
He envelops us, keeps us, protects us

You should know that **I WILL DO ANYTHING**
where you are concerned
because you are the **STAR OF MY LIFE**
and thus He answered me

TONIGHT, as every night,
every day, and forevermore
I will cherish our moments spent together alone,
away from the rest of the world,
in our own **LOVE NEST**

You are **MY DEAREST LOVE**
and because of that
I tend to count the days to the **WEEKEND**
when I'm at last free with you

I truly believe
that **DECEMBER 1ST, 1993** was a preordained date
and one that will forever remain
the dearest of all 365

NEVER-EVER will you be forgotten
or taken for granted by me
for it's beyond truth when I tell you
that **YOU'RE ALWAYS ON MY MIND**

Your **EYES OF LOVE**
burn continually in my mind
serving as a constant reminder
of that which we have together

WHAT I'VE FOUND IN YOU
is more than a dream made real
for **WHENEVER I'M WITH YOU,
THIS FEELING** of **TRUE LOVE**
grows the more

YOUR LOVE is special
because of **WONDERFUL YOU**
and that is only part of the reason
why **I LOVE YOU SO**

MY FIRST LOVE you will forever be,
owing especially to the fact
that you are **TOO GOOD TO BE TRUE**

Allow me to **COMMUNICATE** forthright,
MY MYSTERY LOVER,
because all of **THIS IS TO YOU**
in order that you might better understand

For I also **MEANT IT**
when I said I do, I promise, I will
as you alone are **MY BLESSED CHARM**

And I know
that I definitely made the **RIGHT CHOICE**
when I chose you
now and forevermore

Songs of the Spirit

I just love to write
My songs of the spirit
Whenever I'm in tune
With the Holy Ghost

I write my songs because
I want the world to know
The songs of the spirit
Are in my soul

I just love to write
My songs of the spirit
Because His grace and mercy
Have been good to me

I rejoice in my songs
I rejoice in my soul
So dance to the music
Of the Holy Ghost

I just love to write
My songs of the spirit
Because I see all of myself
And everything in them

The Bible

Can't any other
Find and touch Me
Like the word of God
The good old Bible

It tells me of
Who I am
And how precious I am
In the eyes of God

It tells me of
Why things are
The way they are
And what they ought to be

It tells me of
God's love and plan
His purpose and will
For all my life

Everything I need to know
For my own good
Is in the word of God
The good old Bible

What You've Done for Me

You've done for me
What I couldn't do
And what no one else
Could do for me

You've buried my sins
With your precious blood
You've carried my guilt
Upon your shoulders

As far as the East
Is from the West
So you don't remember
My sins anymore

You've given to me
Another opportunity
To start over again
And live my life for you

I know with you
I cannot go wrong
I know with you
I've got it made

Sincere Wishes

May the joy
And the peace
Of the Lord
Be with You

May His mercy
May His goodness
And His grace
Be upon you

May His spirit
May His light
May His power
Shine upon you

May He keep you
May He guide you
May He hold you
In His arms

My sincerest wish
Is may you be
An overcoming conqueror
Bearing fruits of your salvation

Time

Time is yesterday
Time is today
Time is tomorrow
Time is forever

Time is spring
Time is summer
Time is fall
Time is winter

Time is precious
Time is serious
Everything has a time
Time waits for no one

No one really knows
The hour or day
When our time
Will be no more

So while there's time
Do your very best
And make hay
While the sun yet shines

That's Why

When I was dead
You gave me life
When I was down
You lifted me up

When I was weak
You gave me strength
When I was lost
You showed me the way

That is why, Lord Jesus
You're my friend
That is why, Lord Jesus
You're my Savior

When no one else
Could hear my cries
You were there for me
To answer my prayers

You touched my heart
And made me believe
You touched my soul
And made me whole

Day by Day

Every day by day
Is a brand-new day
Yesterday is gone
And today has come

All of yesterday
With ups and downs
Both good and bad
Is but a memory

Every day by day
Is a brand-new day
For us to do our best
To make things right

One day at a time
One step at a time
Slow and steady
Wins the race

Today is the day
To make things right
Yesterday is gone
Tomorrow is yet to come

Been to Town

When you talk about
Being caught up in the mix
I know what you mean
I've been to town too

When you talk about
No one to care for you
I know what you mean
I've been to town too

When you talk about
Burning up your bridges
I know what you mean
I've been to town too

When you talk about
Being in desperation
I know what you mean
I've been to town too

When you talk about
Being born again
I know what you mean
I've been to town too

Come, Holy Ghost

Come, Holy Ghost
Come take care of me
And help me to be
Whom you want me to be

Come, Holy Ghost
Come lift up my soul
High above the mountains
Way beyond the river

All through the storm
All through the night
Come, Holy Ghost
Come take care of me

Hold onto my hands
And do not let me go
Keep me on my feet
So I do not fall

And when the night falls
When my day is done
Come show me the way
And lead me home

If You Believe

If you believe
You can work wonders
If you believe
You can work miracles

When there's no way
God can make a way
When there's no hope
God can give you hope

If you believe
You can move mountains
If you believe
You can have the victory

If you believe
You can be born again
If you believe
You can live forever

If you confess
That Jesus is Lord
And believe in your heart
That He rose from the dead
You will be saved

I Know Someone

I know someone
Who knows all about
Our every problem
And all our worries

I know someone
Who is our freedom
He is our solution
To the unsolvable

I know someone
Who can do the impossible
He can see the invincible
And move the unmovable

Yeah, I know someone
Who knows exactly
How we feel inside
Because He's been there too

Jesus is that one
Who can give us the victory
We need in our lives
To overcome anything

I Need You

I need you, Lord
To help me walk
Along your way
Of everlasting life

I need you, Lord
To help me persevere
Through all the bad
And the good times too

I need you, Lord
To be with me
That I may know
Everything is alright

I need you, Lord
To walk with me
And talk with me
Along your way

Without you, Lord
I cannot do anything
But I can do all things
Through You who strengthens me

My Buddy

God is my buddy
That I hang out with
Every precious day
Of my life

He knows me very well
And He cares about me
He keeps me from falling
And He provides my needs

God is my buddy
That I can depend on
I can confide in Him
With Him I'm secured

Our friendship is real
His love for me is free
Our friendship is true
His word to me is bond

God is my buddy
That I don't take for granted
He gave His life for me
That I may have life abundantly

New Life

If anyone is in Christ
He is a new creature
The old has gone
The new has come

Since I came to Christ
My life has been transformed
I am born again
And filled with the Spirit

I've played so many games
But I can't play no more
When it comes to Christ
It's a new ballgame

When it comes to Christ
It's a new melody
I have a new song
Inside of my heart

When it comes to Christ
We must live by faith
The life I lived before
I lived by sight

Getting Paid

Whenever I can witness
About the Good News
To someone else
That's how I get paid

Whenever I can reach out
To someone else
Who is in need
That's how I get paid

Whenever I can make
Someone else's day
With nothing but a smile
That's how I get paid

Whenever I can help
People to get along
Despite their differences
That's how I get paid

Whenever I can be
A blessing to others
As others have been to me
That's how I get paid

Give Thanks

I give thanks to God
For the many things
That He has done
And is still doing for me

I give thanks to God
For transforming my life
For renewing my mind
For making me His own

I give thanks to God
And magnify His name
I give thanks to God
And glorify His name

I love you, my Lord
For you first loved me
While I was yet a sinner
Christ died for me

I give thanks to God
And magnify His name
I give thanks to God
And glorify His name

Handiwork

The beauty of the flowers
The fresh leaves of spring
After the winter is gone
Are the handiwork of God

The falling rain drops
The misty dew drops
And the flaky snow flakes
Are the handiwork of God

The sunshine of the day
The moonlight of the night
And the twinkling stars above
Are the handiwork of God

The beast of the fields
The flying creatures and birds
And the fishes of the seas
Are the handiwork of God

Everywhere I look
Myself being inclusive
All that I can see
Is the handiwork of God

Give to Me

Give to me a mind
That has been made up
Give to me a will
That will never give up

Give to me your shine
That I may see
Give to me your spirit
That is your seal

Give to me my dreams
That my heart desires
Give to me my needs
That you cannot deny

Give to me your power
That I may be obedient
Give to me your peace
That I may be content

Give to me a life
That is very fruitful
Give to me a life
That is very thankful

Coming Again

Jesus is coming
He is coming again
To claim His own
Unto Himself

The signs of the times
Are there to see
To let us know
He's coming again

No one really knows
The hour or day
When the King of Kings
Is coming again

Like the days of Noah
Like a thief in the night
The Lord of Lords
Is coming again

So people get ready
Jesus is coming
He's coming again
Don't be left behind

I Must Tell Somebody

I must tell somebody
About the Good News
So they might be able
To tell somebody else

I must tell somebody
Like somebody else told me
To taste of the Lord
And see that the Lord is good

I must tell somebody
That God so loved everybody
That whoever believes in Him
Will have everlasting life

I must tell somebody
That if they've tried everything
And nothing seems to work
Give Jesus Christ a chance

I must tell somebody
Now is the appointed time
Today is the day of salvation
Tomorrow may be too late

Children

Children of today
Really don't know
Right from wrong
Or which way to go

Babies are having babies
Children are killing children
And all the grownups
Don't have the answers

Children of today
Grow up so fast
That they don't have
Childhood anymore

We owe it to them
To help them have
Respect for themselves
And respect for life

God help the children
God bless the children
God help the children
Can't no one else do

Our Love

Your love for me
Is my enticement
Your love for me
Is my enchantment

My love for you
Is more than you know
My love for you
Is more than love

Your love for me
Is my upliftment
Your love for me
Is my ecstasy

My love for you
Is not in songs
My love for you
Is in myself

You've become so much
Another part of me
That I cannot imagine
My life without you

Happy Birthday

Happy birthday to you
My very dear one
Who I now consider
As my bona-fide wife

Being married to you
Has helped me to grow
In the knowledge and experience
Of what love is all about

Your birthday is one day
For me to let you know
That my love for you
Grows with every new day

I'm more than blessed
To have a wife like you
It's no wonder I love you
More than words can say

I wish you the best
And many happy returns
Long life and good life
And life more abundantly

My Daughter

My daughter is precious to me
She is my first child
And she is the princess
Of my royal family

Her countenance is strong
And she is very healthy
Her eyes are so bright
She is my chocolate baby

Whenever she smiles
She blows me away
Whenever she cries
She makes me worry

She has made me grow up
In a lot of ways
I'm now learning to be
A responsible parent

The prayer of my heart
Is for the Lord to help me
To always be there
Whenever she needs me

Every Day

Every day by day
I'm thankful to know
That your love for me
Is ever so strong

You take me places
That's so intimate
You take me places
That's so passionate

No one else could ever
Know me so well
No one else could ever
Love me so dearly

Every day by day
I'm thankful to know
That your love for me
Is ever so strong

You deserve all my love
And I'll always love you
In the only way I know
Every day of my life

To the Mother of My Child

I am so happy
And more than thankful
That you're the mother
Of my child

I've always wanted
To have a family
Like I now have
With you and our child

Whenever I look at you
And at our child
Then I truly know
That I've been blessed

I'm so happy for us
And I'm so proud of you
After all you went through
To be the mother of my child

My prayer for us
Is for God to enable us
To be the parents that
He would have us be

Happy Anniversary

If you must know
What's on my mind
It is the same thing
I have in my heart

This is the day
For me to remind you
Of what you mean to me
On our wedding anniversary

Though I don't always give you
The compliments due to you
But one thing I know
You mean everything to me

With every passing day
You become more beautiful to me
And more precious to me
Beyond my hopes and dreams

I wish us the very best
Of a happy anniversary
And of what we have together
Today and for always

She's Only Got Eyes for Me

My wife don't play that
She ain't down with that
Don't even think about it
She's only got eyes for me

Back in the days
When all the guys
Were always in her face
She never gave them a play

Little did they know
That her golden mind
Had already been made up
She's only got eyes for me

How I'm so proud of her
The way she makes me feel
I'm the only one for her
She's only got eyes for me

I don't have to worry
Or look over my shoulder
Don't even think about it
She's only got eyes for me

PART III

Springs of Adventure

Let us live again
Within that sunny world
Far away from this world
That slaves for materialism

*   *   *

Come go with me
And please welcome yourself
Within that sunny world
Of the springs of adventure

Pause!

Read the simple words
On each bud of page
Catch the loaded quotes
Along the theme of adventure

Can you feel the rhythm
And read between the lines?
Can you float and dance
To the tune of adventure?

There's no eloquent phrase
There's no sparked metaphor
Only through modest simplicity
That the vibes of adventure
Manifest themselves with

Springs of adventure
Is but another window
Into the very deep within
Relative to all beings

As the name implies, "Springs of Adventure" sets the insight of experience into the golden frame of quotations. It quotes and speaks not with the cold voice of reason, but with the glow and warmth of a full heart. Mere intellectual wisdom isolates and separates, but the springs of adventure reconcile and unite.

Springs of adventure are the wisdom of many and the wit of one. They are the salty sentences which precipitate some nebulous truth and brightness into the minds and souls of beings.

In the springs of adventure, there are to be found the accounts of countless and interlocked generations, handed on from old to young. Through springs of adventure, the soul sees through the commonplace of daily life, far into the dim mysteries of existence.

If wisdom is more than cleverness, and if quotable quotes belong to wisdom, it must follow that the springs of adventure become beneficial. The springs of adventure see through the brightness and light that lie in the depth of beings and so, they identify with this brightness.

Learning is the eye of the mind. But so many of us perish through vain learning. A learned being is like a well-cut stone. A single day among the learned lasts longer than the longest life of the ignorant. No one is born learned. But learning without understanding is useless. Because what we do not understand, we do not possess.

In the way of the absolute, the wise being is that being who realizes that there is no end to knowledge and knowing. Until the very hour of our departure, we never stop learning.

Trust in the Lord
With all your heart
And lean not on
Your own understanding.
In all your ways
Acknowledge Him
And He will make
Your paths straight.

—Proverbs 3:5–6

Springs of Adventure

1. The fear of the Lord
   Is the beginning of wisdom

   —Psalm 111:10

2. True understanding
   Is in endless expression
   And not on imposition

3. Heaven must first be in us
   Before we can be in heaven

4. In the spiritual world
   No one is permitted
   To think and will in one way
   And to
   Speak and act in another

5. Of all sacred acts
   Prayer comes first

6. The end of times is coming
   The only reason for its coming
   Is that it already exists

7. Anyone who is afraid
   Of the winds or clouds
   Will never truly embark
   On a true adventure

8. Every good gift
   And every perfect gift
   Comes from up above

   —James 1:17

9.   Nothing is farther
     Than earth from heaven
     And nothing is nearer
     Than heaven to earth

10. The human heart
     At whatever age
     Only opens to the heart
     That opens in return

11. An adult is one
     Who has ceased to grow vertically
     But not horizontally

12. In youth we learn
     In age we understand

13. Prosperity is a great teacher
     But adversity is greater
     Possession pampers the mind
     While privation trains
     And strengthens it

14. Without love in us
     We will be spiritless

15. To believe everything
     Is too much
     And to believe nothing
     Ain't enough

16. Of all our many acts
     Repentance is divine
     The greatest of faults
     Is to be conscious of none

17. To err is human
    But to forgive is divine

18. When all else is lost
    The future still remains

19. Love never possesses
    Neither would it be possessed
    It is just so sufficient
    And content within itself

20. We come and we cry
    And that is life
    We yawn and we go
    And that is death

21. Out of eternity
    A new day is born
    And into eternity
    A night will return

22. We attract hearts
    By the qualities we display
    And we retain them
    By the qualities we possess

23. Abstract thoughts
    Provide us knowledge
    Beyond the ordinary scope
    Of objective experience

24. To youth is the future
    To age is the fruitage
    Of experience

25. Life is always half-spent
    Before we even know
    What it is

26. If we make ourselves understood
    We must be speaking correctly

27. Humility is the foundation
    Of all the virtues

28. A well-bred being
    Has no pretensions

29. As we advance in life
    We learn the limits
    Of our abilities

30. Man has his will
    But woman has her way

31. Understanding hearts
    Search for knowledge
    But ill-willing hearts
    Aspire to foolishness

32. It is far better to be
    The one we ought to be
    Than the one we incline to be

33. That which is unjust
    Can profit no one
    And that which is just
    Can harm no one

34. Whoever falls into sin is human
    Whoever grieves at it is godly
    Whoever boasts in it is evil

35. It is not what we do alone
    But also what we do not do
    For which we are accountable

36. The only good is knowledge
    The only evil is ignorance

37. Whoever thinks that
    He does not need others
    Has simply become unreasonable

38. Young love is like a flame
    Often pretty, hot, and fierce
    Usually, it is only a flicker
    Older love is more disciplined
    Like the coal that's deep burning
    It is more often unquenchable

39. Sleep
    Is like the nearest relative
    Of death

40. I can forgive
    But I can never forget
    Is another way of saying
    That I will not forgive

41. Only the wise know
    The true strength of kindness
    For the learned know
    That kind acts are not
    Always returned in kind

42. Saying yes to drugs
    Is absolutely nothing
    But voluntary madness

43. As we grow in wisdom
    We pardon more freely

44. Poetry heals the wound
    Inflicted upon the soul
    By reason

45. Those who complain most
    Are most to be complained of

46. The most lost day of all
    Is the day we don't laugh

47. Poets are for always
    Indebted to the universe
    Paying interests and fines
    On happiness and sorrows

48. If our expectations
    Stand unfulfilled
    Then we keep on hoping

49. The future enters us
    So as to transform itself in us
    Long before it even happens

50. We discover in ourselves
    What others hide from us
    And we recognize in others
    What we hide from ourselves

51. Most of us
    Are not always what we seem
    And we are seldom better

52. There are two ways
    Of meeting difficulties
    Either we alter them
    Or we alter ourselves
    To meet them

53. Life is like a mirror
    If we show ourselves in it
    It will reflect our image

54. Good is the content
    Of what we call happiness

55. Love can be blind at times
    But its eyesight
    Can be restored in marriage

56. The greatest thoughts
    Are simply expressed
    For in their simplicity
    Lies their clarity

57. There's no human endeavor
That can fully answer
Our hearts' ultimate longings

58. The word of God
Will stand a thousand readings
Whoever goes over them
Time and time again
Is sure to find new wonders there

59. A politician
Thinks of the next election
While a statesman
Thinks of the next generation

60. It is much easier
To know mankind in general
Than in trying to know
A being individually

61. There is one person
Who is wiser than anybody
And that person is everybody

62. There is no other beauty
That is like the beauty within

63. The most universal quality
Is diversity

64. That which is spoken
Is too soon forgotten
But that which is written
Is forever abiding

65. Everything great
    Is not always good
    But all good things
    Are always great

66. There is no creature without love
    And there is no perfect love
    Without adequate jealousy

67. Heard melodies are sweet
    But the unheard melodies
    Are by far the sweetest

68. Talent alone
    Cannot make a writer
    There must also be
    A being behind the book

69. In prosperity
    Our friends know us
    In adversity
    We know our friends

—Epictetus

70. Whoever does nothing
    Need hope for nothing
    Whoever has no cross
    Will have no crown

71. Prudent use of knowledge
    Constitutes wisdom

72. Fame like a river
    Is narrowest where bred
    And broadest afar off

73. There is a spirit within us
    Who breathes that divine fire
    By which we are animated

74. Whoever realizes not
    That learning has no end
    Will be very apt to think
    That he knows everything

75. We grow
    By the obstacles
    We do overcome

76. We should love our calling
    With passion
    For it is the meaning
    Of our coming

77. If we do not hope
    We will never find that
    Which is beyond our hopes

78. Along the Milky Way
    There exists the search
    Not only for excitement
    But also for the exquisite delight
    For adventure

79. The ocean of life
    Is full of marvelous promises
    But we must be aware
    That there are storms and tempests
    And dangerous pirates as well

80. The gift of God is life
    The hope of evil is destruction

81. The spirit is born old
    But it grows younger
    That is the comedy of life
    In contrast, however,
    The body is born young
    And it grows older
    That is the tragedy of life

82. If we run after wit
    We will succeed in catching folly

83. The other world
    Is a dwelling place
    Of which this our world
    Is the vestibule

84. Those given to darkness
    Cannot understand judgment
    But those who walk in righteousness
    Can understand things as they are

85. Self-confidence
    Is the ability to endure misfortune
    Without looking for someone to blame

86. Who can tell where love begins
    Much less of where it ends?
    Perhaps it is better expressed
    When we safely say that
    The beginning of love has no end

87. Evil is easy
    Its forms are infinite
    But goodness is unique

88. The biggest mistake
    That we can make
    Is to worry about mistakes

89. What are clouds?
    But an excuse from the skies
    What is life?
    But an escape from death

                              —James Clavell

90. Honest bread is well
    But the temptation
    Lies in the butter

91. When we swell with glory
    Our overweening pride
    Is soon abashed

92. God does not look
    To see if our hearts are full
    What God looks at
    Is to see if our hearts are clean

93. We cannot do evil to others
    Without doing it to ourselves

94. Everything noble today
    Is fast vanishing away
    Wickedness now calls itself goodness
    Ignorance now calls itself awareness

Foolishness now calls itself wisdom
And man's own understanding
Now calls itself freedom

95.   Whatever liberates our spirit
Without giving us the mastery
And control over ourselves
Is very very dangerous
And can also become destructive

96.   Every one of us
Lends the color of our understanding
To our surroundings

97.   All human beings are
But a spark of being
On an adventure through time
Until the law comes touching us

98.   Of all vain things
Excuses are the vainest

99.   The good has one enemy
And that enemy is evil
Evil has two enemies
Which are good and itself

100. Good talk is like good scenery
Continuous, yet constantly varying
Full of the charm of novelty
As well as surprises

101. All change is not growth
As all movement is not forward

102. Nature is an infinite sphere
Of which the center is everywhere
And the circumference is nowhere

103. We cannot live better
Than in seeking to become better
Neither can we live more agreeably
Than in having a clear conscience

104. We are all born to love
It is the principle of existence
As well as its constitution

105. The universe is one city
Full of beloved ones
Who are human by nature
And are endeared to each other

106. The first condition of private prayer
Is to recognize that solitude
Is the stronghold of the strong
And to provide for its place in life

107. The love of humanity
Is the whole of morality
This by itself
Is goodness and humanism
As well as
The social conscience

108. A good deed is never lost
It is a treasure laid up
And guarded for the doer's need

For every noble activity
Makes room for itself

109. If we know the beginning well
The end will not trouble us

110. A true and good teacher
Can influence eternity
Without actually knowing
Where the influence stops

111. No being was ever
So much deceived by another
As by itself

112. There is so much good
In the worst of us
And there is so much bad
In the best of us that
It ill behooves any of us
To find fault with the rest of us

—Edward Wallis

113. Young men think
That old men are fools
But the older ones know
That the younger ones are the fools

114. We give little
When we give of our possessions
It is when we give of ourselves
That we truly give

115. Insanity is not a distant empire
Our ordinary life borders upon it
And we often cross the frontier
In some part of our nature

116. Birds get entangled by their feet
Humans get entangled by their tongues

117. There are few things
That never go out of style
And a feminine woman
Is one of them

118. A wonderful stream
Is the river of time
As it runs through the river of tears
With a faultless rhythm
And with a musical rhyme
So it blends with the ocean of years

119. Childhood is like a butterfly
Intent on burning its white wings
In the flames of youth

120. Procrastination
Is a disease of the will

121. Men always want to be
A woman's first love
While women like to be
A man's last romance

122. Whenever we receive a good turn
We should never forget it
And whenever we do a good turn
We should never remember it

123. It is some relief to weep
Grief is satisfied
And it is also
Carried off by tears

124. It is easy to flatter
But it is harder to praise

125. The earth has no sorrow
That heaven cannot heal

126. Destiny is not a matter of chance
It is a matter of choice
It is not a thing to be waited for
It is a thing to be achieved

127. Men love little and often
While women love much and rarely

128. An old story
Does not open the ears
As much as a new one does

129. It is our nature to err
But only a fool perseveres in error

130. To be conscious of one's ignorance
Is a great step to knowledge

131. Strange how much we've got to know
Before we realize how little we know

132. No one should be despaired of
As long as there is life
There is hope still

133. Drug abuse is illing
It not only destroys the health
It also dismounts the mind
It is lascivious and impudent
And for the worst part of all
It brings about poverty
And makes human beings become unbeings

134. Doing an injury in any way
Puts one below
And revenging an injury in any way
Makes one even
But forgiving an injury in all ways
Sets one above

135. It is only imperfection
That complains of what is imperfect
The more perfect we are
The more gentle and quiet
And the more understanding we become
Towards the defects of others

136. We have indeed found wealth
When we find happiness
In unbought peace of mind

137. Self-knowledge
Is the true beginning
Of self-improvement

138. We should find some degree of joy daily
For life gives no assurance of tomorrow

139. God does not in any way
Expect the perfection of action
What God expects from us
Is the perfection of intention
And the offering of true obedience

140. All the flowers of tomorrow
Are in the seeds of today

141. Love is a circle
Without ending
Never narrow
And always bending

142. We should never let our yesterdays
Use up our today

143. A true prayer
Requires more of the heart
Than of words

144. Kindness is the ability
To love people
More than they deserve

145. No amount of good deeds
Can make us good persons
We must be good
Before we can do good

146. God comforts us
Not to make us comfortable
But to make us comforters

147. It is only the fear of God
That is able to deliver us
From the fear of man

148. The truest end of life
Is to know this:
That life never ends

149. As rain restores the earth
So hope restores the spirit

150. A hug is a great gift
One size fits all
And it is easy to exchange

151. We must never be afraid to venture
We must believe with all our being
That life is really worth living
And when our belief is rooted in truth
It will help to create the fact

152. The secret of life is that
It is God-given

153. The true disciples of Christ
Are not those who know most
But those who love most

154. All people smile
In the same language

155. Worship renews the spirit
Just as sleep renews the body

156. We should love those
Who point out our faults
But we seldom do

157. We should learn
To speak kind words
Nobody resents them

158. God loves every one of us
As if there were only one of us

159. Commit to the Lord
Whatever you do
And your plans will succeed

160. Unconditional love
Is the only condition
With which one should love

161. Christianity is not only
Believing in something
It is also believing
In receiving somebody

162. "To be born again"
     Is more than just believing
     It is knowing the Lord

163. Life is not lived in full
     Until one has been
     Spiritually born again

164. In the spiritual realm
     Every last thing
     Cannot and should not
     Be reasoned out with logic

165. The cross at Calvary
     Is the focal point
     Of Christianity
     And of divine revelation

166. Keep your face to the sunshine
     And you will not see the shadow

167. Salvation is not of ourselves
     Neither is it of the church
     It is not of man
     But of divine providence

168. The confession of Jesus
     Crystallizes our faith in him
     And waxes us stronger in the Lord

169. Every time we sin
     It separates us from God
     Every time we sin
     It weakens our will
     Every time we sin
     It holds us more captive

170. To believe in Christ
     Means to confess our faith in Him
     To rely and be dependent on Him
     And to totally commit oneself to Him

171. The heart is ever restless
     Until it finds rest in God

172. Whenever the devil
     Taunts us with our past
     We should remind him
     Of his future

173. Believers don't have to worry
     About forgiving themselves
     Because they have already
     Been forgiven by God

But all good things
Must come to an end
And so,
One must move onward
Into the space left behind
By one's own conclusions